PLAYTIME PUZZLES

HIGHLIGHTS PRESS

Honesdale, Pennsylvania

Welcome, Hidden Pictures® Puzzlers!

When you finish a puzzle, check it off √ . Good luck, and happy puzzling!

Contents

Contents

Two Scoops!

hockey stick

pennant

artist's
brush

envelope

mitten

carrot

sock

seashell

banana

eyeglasses

slice of pizza

sock

toothbrush

seashell

Round and Round

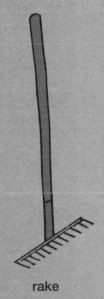
rake

balloon

Illustrated by Dave Klug

Great Skate

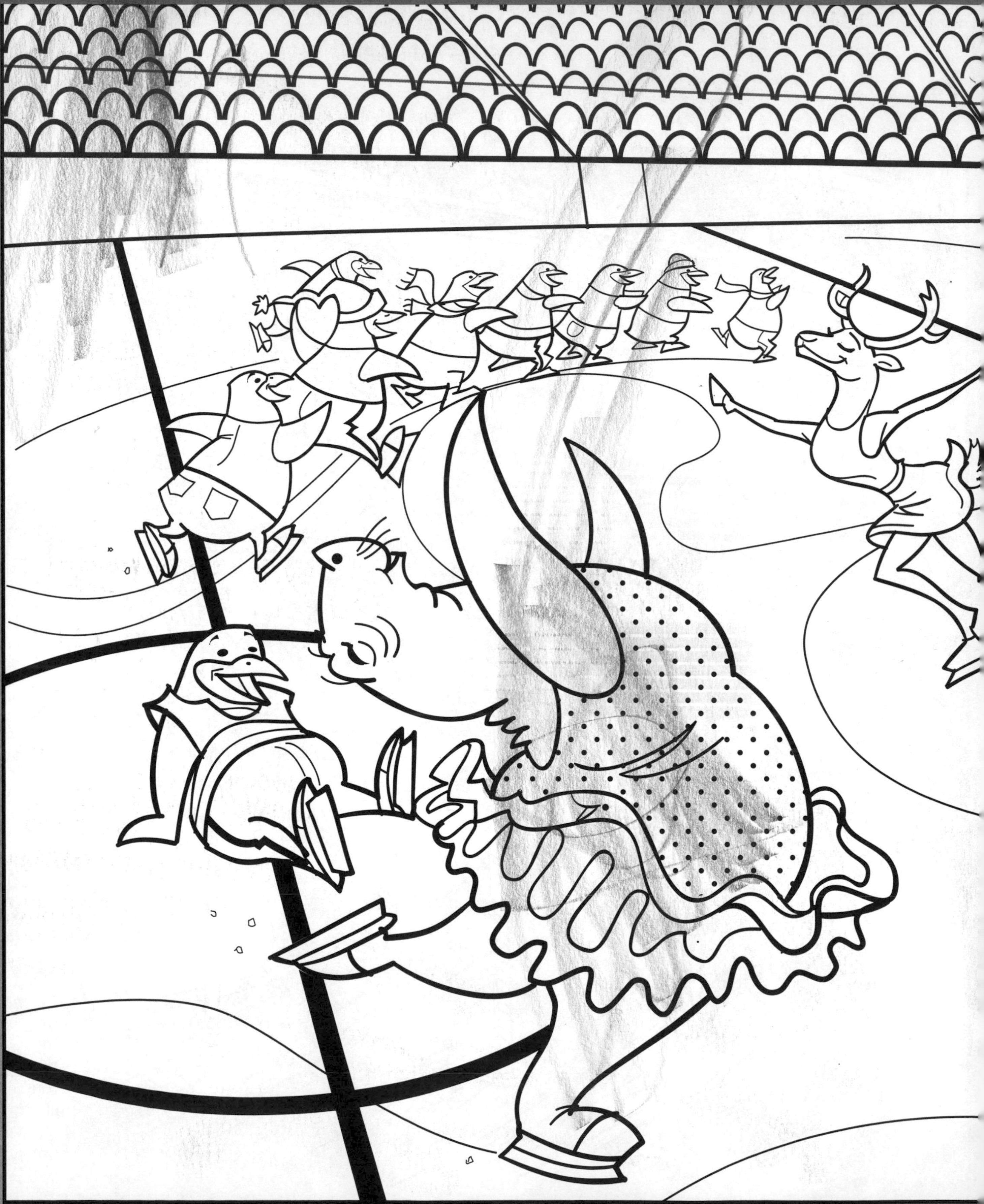

That's Tall!

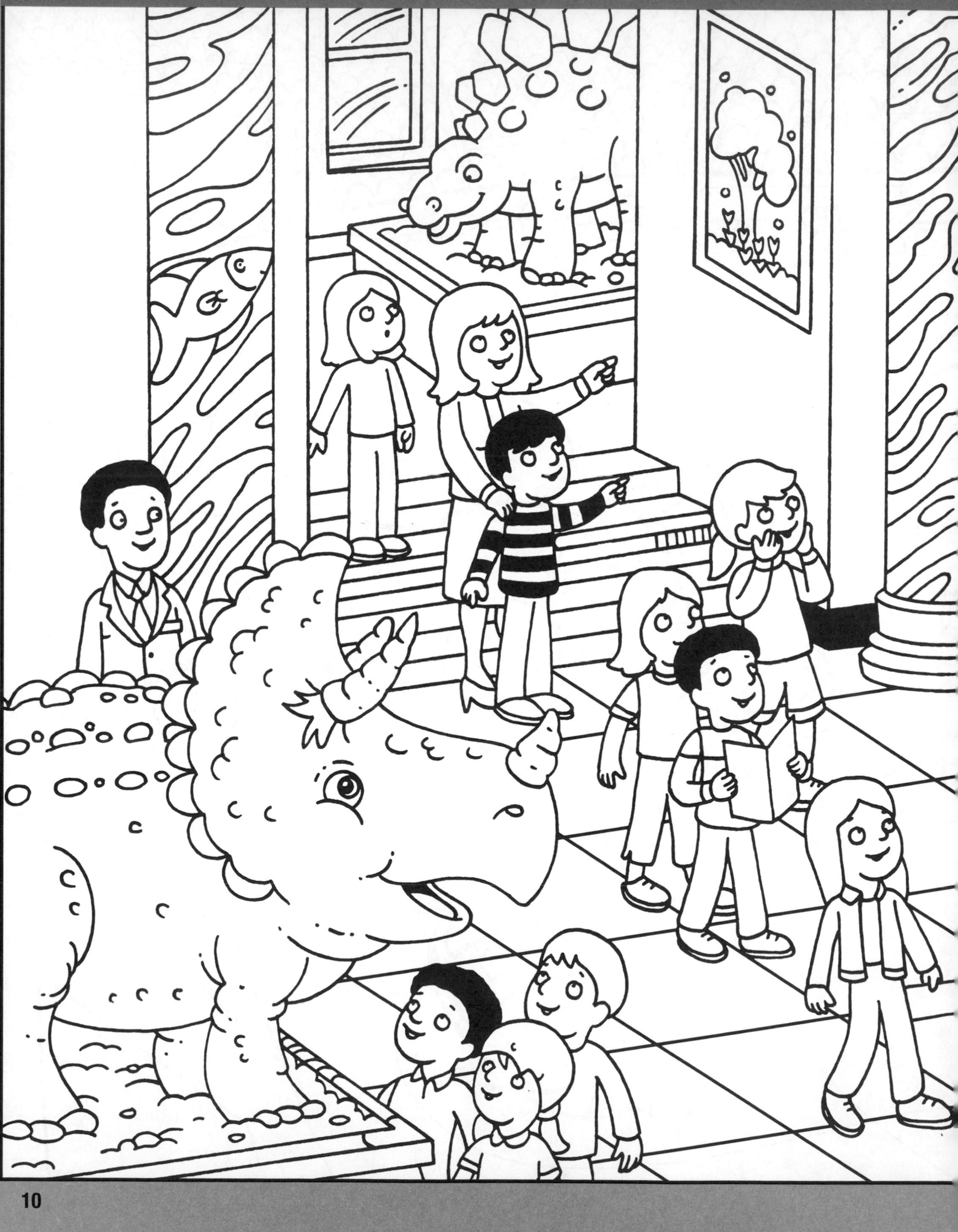

Band Practice

balloon

cane

lemon

ice-cream cone

comb

banana

crown

ruler

crescent
moon

muffin

microphone

mushroom

Music Makers

magnifying
glass

mop

mitten

mug

Illustrated by Kelly Kennedy

13

saltshaker

crayon

baseball

crescent moon

spoon

slice of pizza

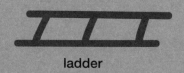
ladder

banana

boot

envelope

cheese

sailboat

Tall, Tall Tower

horseshoe

mug

fried egg

bird

Illustrated by Mike Moran

15

Gym Meet

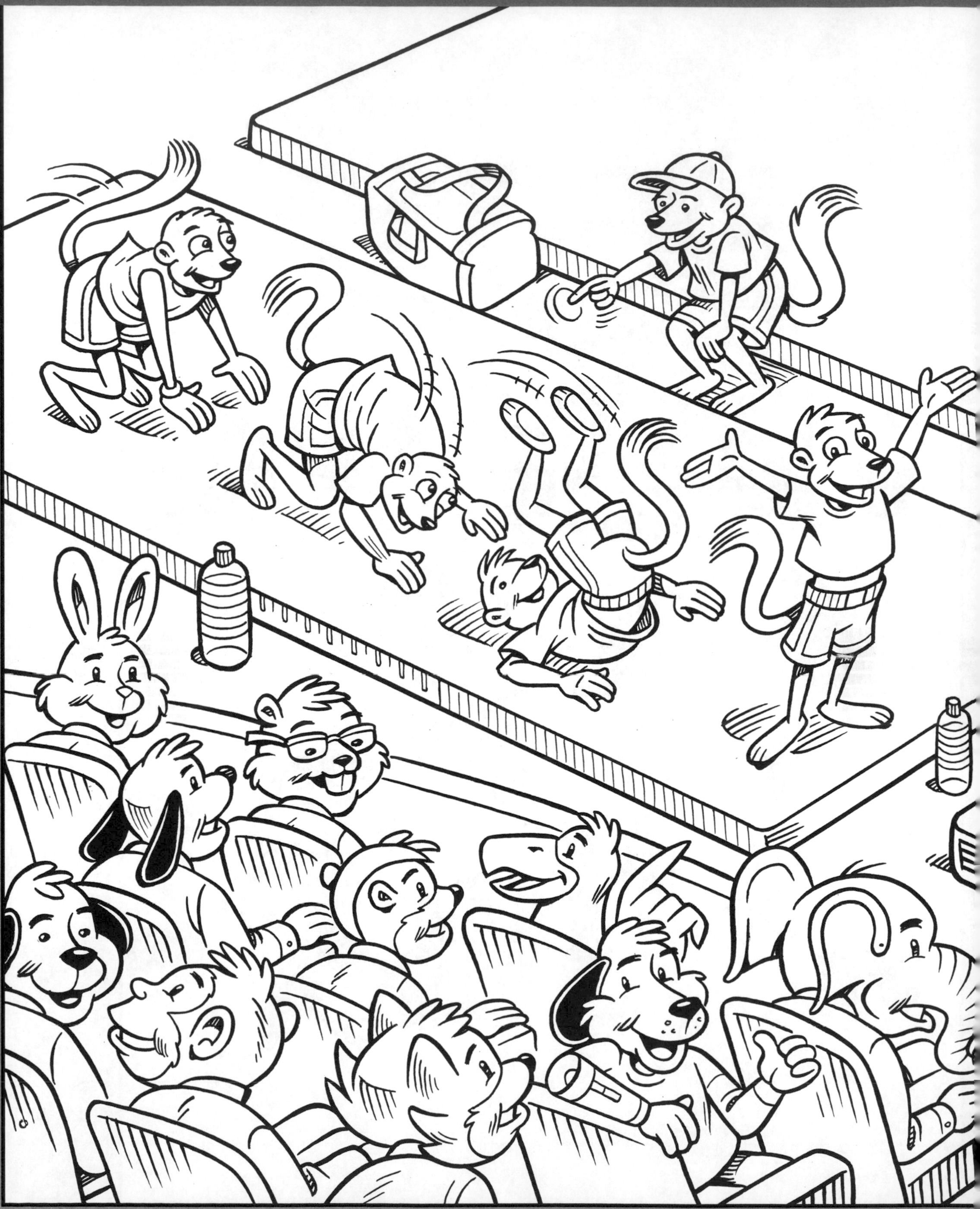

Two Points

sock

balloon

pillowcase

hairbrush

peanut

measuring tape

envelope

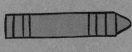

crayon

18

mitten

airplane

rug

cat

Sweet Dreams!

mug

sock

lock

cane

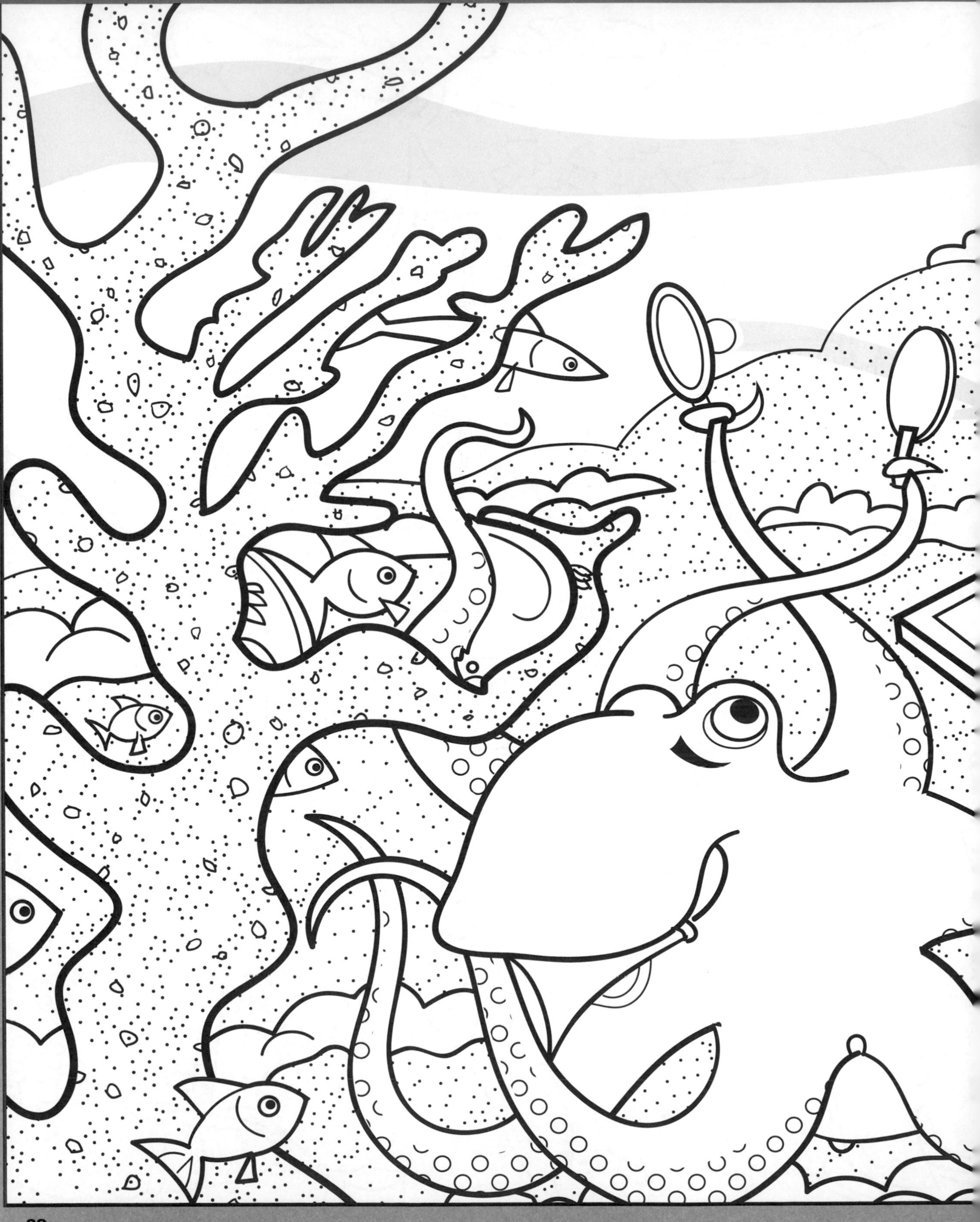

At the Fair

flower

football

fork

flowerpot

frying pan

fish

four-leaf
clover

flashlight

cupcake

crescent
moon

dish

corn

fish

Story Time

spoon

snowflake

party horn

Illustrated by Jannie Ho

City Slide

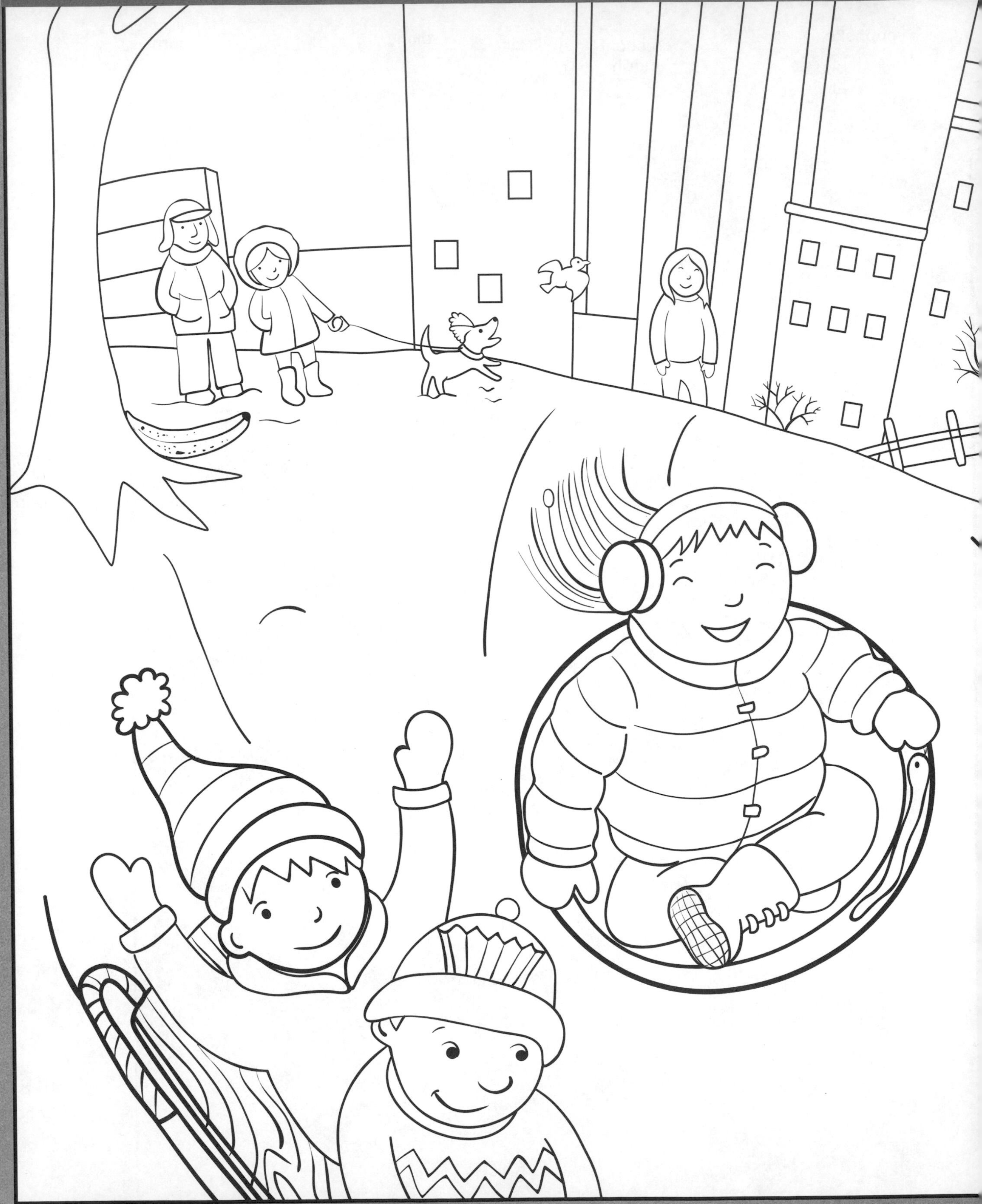

Illustrated by David Helton

Balloon Fun

broccoli

slice of
bread

banana

button

boot

bell

book

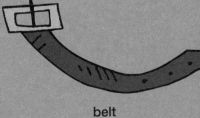

belt

30

airplane

heart

pail

jacket

tennis racket

cane

dart

Ants Dance

nail

31

One More Piece!

cheese

butterfly

broccoli

balloon

celery

acorn

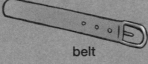
belt

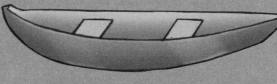
canoe

lime

heart

belt

balloon

Apple Picking

football

paper clip

fork

star

A New Home

basketball

doughnut

sailboat

screwdriver

skateboard

watermelon

seashell

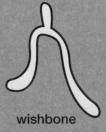
wishbone

horseshoe

letter

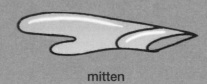
mitten

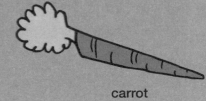
carrot

Catch of the Day

fork

toothbrush

fried egg

candy cane

Illustrated by Ron Zalme

Smooth Sailing

dog bone

baseball bat

mitten

ladybug

snake

heart

clock

hairbrush

48

786C-05

Let's Go Golfing!
(pages 4–5)

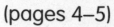

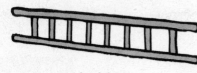

teacup

book

ladder

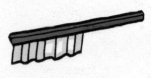

cookie

toothbrush

glove

ice pop

sock

ladle

ring

ruler

artist's brush

786C-05

Great Skate
(pages 8–9)

needle

horn

balloon

paper clip

crescent
moon

heart

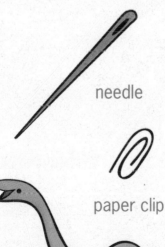

banana

snake

slice of pie

toothbrush

bell

teacup

That's Tall!
(pages 10–11)

fish

carrot

pencil

golf club

crescent moon

fried egg

ring

comb

ice-cream bar

hammer

baseball bat

toothbrush

Gym Meet
(pages 16–17)

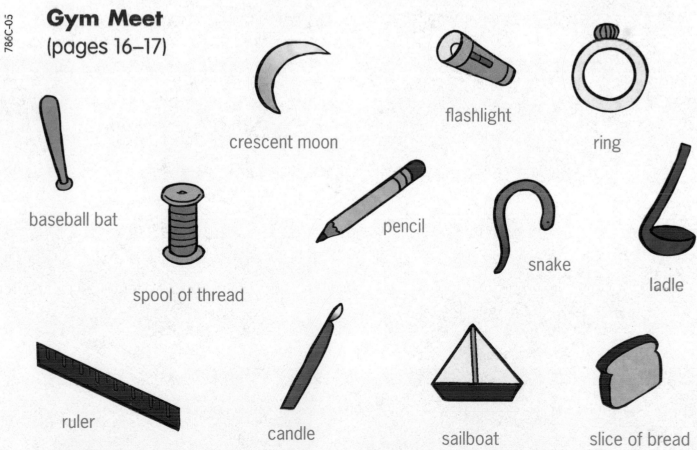

crescent moon

flashlight

ring

baseball bat

pencil

snake

ladle

spool of thread

ruler

candle

sailboat

slice of bread

Horsing Around
(pages 20–21)

teacup

canoe

heart

wristwatch

mitten

funnel

toothpaste

glove

toothbrush

caterpillar

comb

feather

Let's Play!
(pages 22–23)

heart

baseball cap

frying pan

shoe

horn

bell

teacup

candle

ice-cream cone

toothbrush

ring

chicken

City Slide
(pages 26–27)

banana

candy cane

comb

cupcake

potato

peanut

envelope

loaf of bread

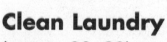

yo-yo

slice of watermelon

postage stamp

snake

Clean Laundry
(pages 28–29)

ruler

kite

book

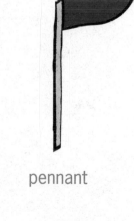
pennant

banana

sock

feather

sailboat

horseshoe

cupcake

golf club

mitten

Set Sail
(pages 32–33)

slice of pie

flag

nail

fork

balloon

pencil

crescent moon

hockey
stick

toothbrush

letter

snail

cupcake

Cave Explorers
(pages 34–35)

paper clip

feather

umbrella

fish

fork

crescent moon

comb

ice-cream cone

saw

artist's brush

turtle

toothbrush

I ♥ You!
(pages 38–39)

baseball bat

crescent moon

envelope

crown

doughnut

wedge of apple

wishbone

seashell

muffin

candle

bell

ring

What a Hoot!
(pages 40–41)

worm

spoon

banana

glove

book

wristwatch

balloon

cane

crayon

slice of bread

horseshoe

comb

Highlights™ Highlights™

Hidden Pictures® Hidden Pictures®

Highlights™ Highlights™

Hidden Pictures® Hidden Pictures®

Highlights™ Highlights™

Hidden Pictures® Hidden Pictures®

Highlights™ Highlights™

Hidden Pictures® Hidden Pictures®

Highlights™ Highlights™

Hidden Pictures® Hidden Pictures®

Highlights™ Highlights™

Hidden Pictures® Hidden Pictures®

Highlights™ Highlights™

Hidden Pictures® Hidden Pictures®

Ready or Not!
(pages 44–45)

ruler

fish

cupcake

spoon

mitten

toothbrush

carrot

tack

heart

paintbrush

banana

flag

Follow the Leader
(pages 46–47)

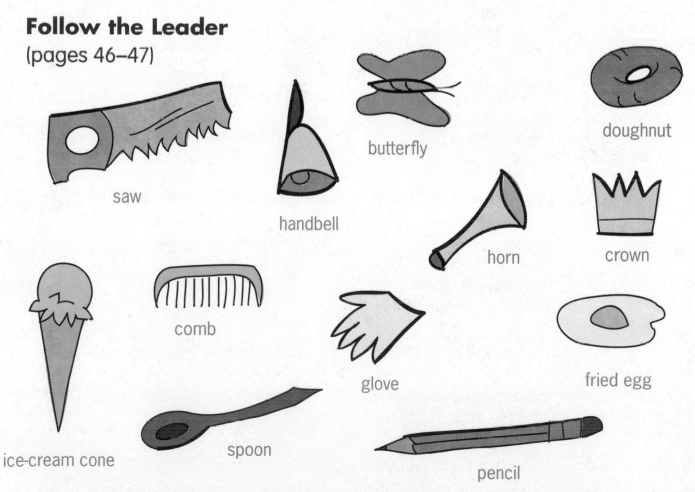

butterfly

doughnut

saw

handbell

horn

crown

ice-cream cone

comb

glove

fried egg

spoon

pencil

Highlights™

Hidden Pictures®

Highlights™ Highlights™
Hidden Pictures® Hidden Pictures®
Highlights™ Highlights™
Hidden Pictures® Hidden Pictures®
Highlights™ Highlights™
Hidden Pictures® Hidden Pictures®
Highlights™ Highlights™
Hidden Pictures® Hidden Pictures®
Highlights™ Highlights™
Hidden Pictures® Hidden Pictures®
Highlights™ Highlights™
Hidden Pictures® Hidden Pictures®
Highlights™ Highlights™
Hidden Pictures® Hidden Pictures®

Warming Up
(pages 50–51)

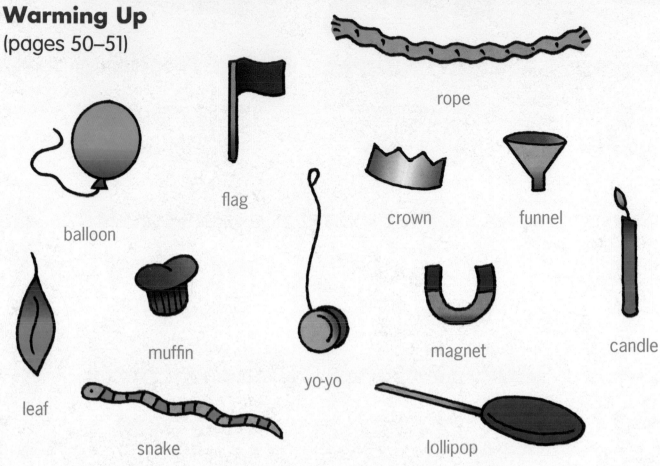

rope

balloon

flag

crown

funnel

candle

leaf

muffin

yo-yo

magnet

snake

lollipop

Taco Tuesday
(pages 52–53)

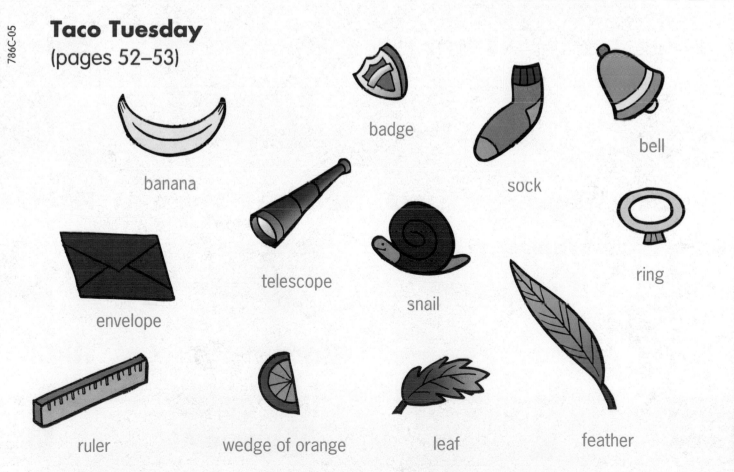

banana

badge

sock

bell

envelope

telescope

snail

ring

ruler

wedge of orange

leaf

feather

Highlights

Hidden Pictures

Highlights
Hidden Pictures
Highlights
Hidden Pictures
Highlights
Hidden Pictures
Highlights
Hidden Pictures
Highlights
Hidden Pictures
Highlights
Hidden Pictures

A Perfect Pumpkin
(pages 56–57)

 seashell

 ring

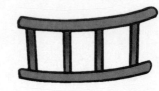 ladder

 banana

 toothbrush

 spoon

 pencil

 feather

 comb

 glove

 sock

 magnifying glass

786C-05

Fresh Picked
(pages 58–59)

 cupcake

 funnel

 bell

 clock

 cane

 ruler

crescent moon

 heart

 balloon

 four-leaf clover

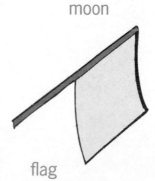 flag

 ladle

Back and Forth
(pages 62–63)

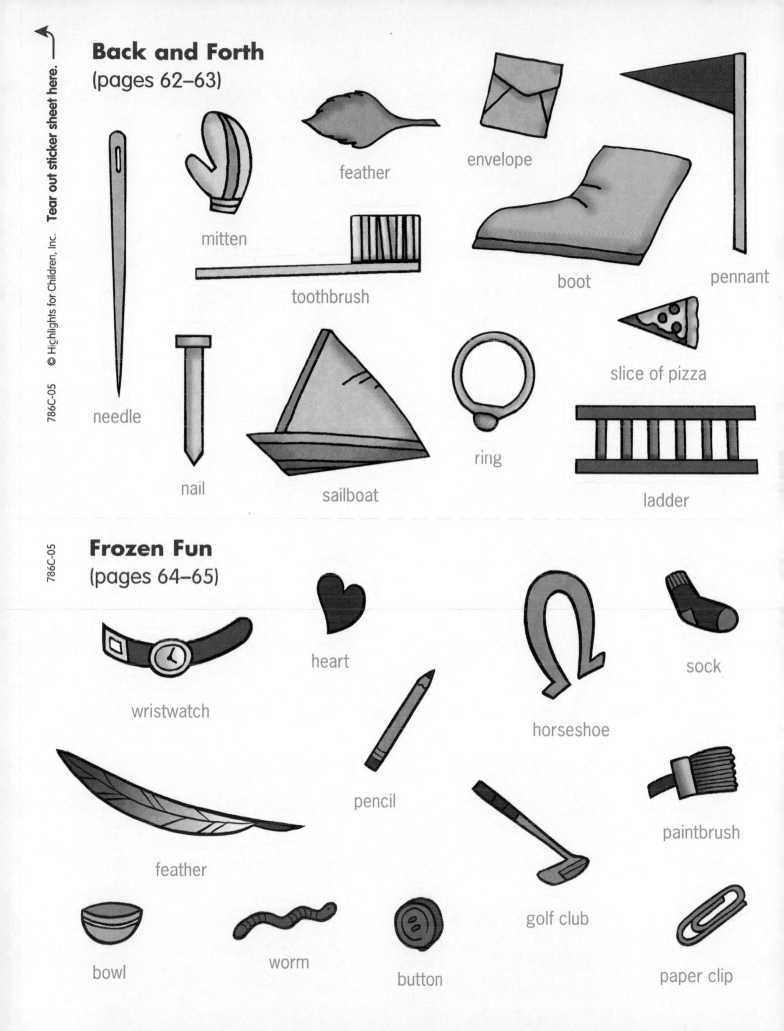

feather

envelope

mitten

boot

pennant

toothbrush

needle

slice of pizza

nail

sailboat

ring

ladder

Frozen Fun
(pages 64–65)

heart

horseshoe

sock

wristwatch

pencil

paintbrush

feather

golf club

bowl

worm

button

paper clip

Pony Rides
(pages 68–69)

mitten

hockey stick

saw

flag

wishbone

crown

baby's bottle

teacup

hammer

broccoli

ice-cream cone

pencil

Wild Workout
(pages 74–75)

heart

pencil

toothbrush

golf club

fish

shoe

banana

crown

slice of pie

bell

feather

ice-cream cone

Having a Ball
(pages 76–77)

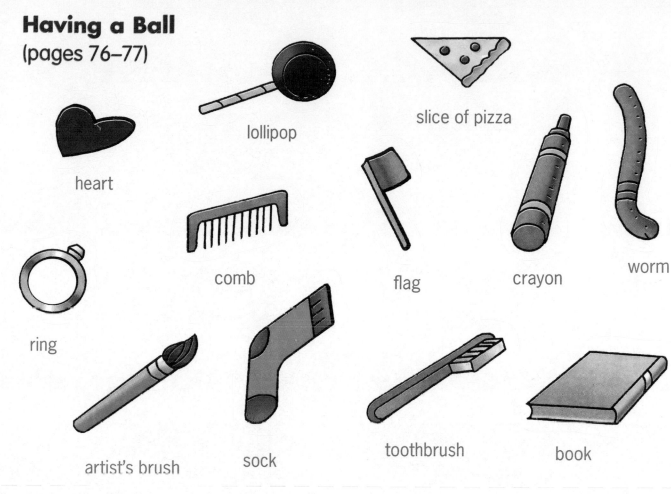

heart

lollipop

slice of pizza

comb

flag

crayon

worm

ring

artist's brush

sock

toothbrush

book

Helping Out
(pages 82–83)

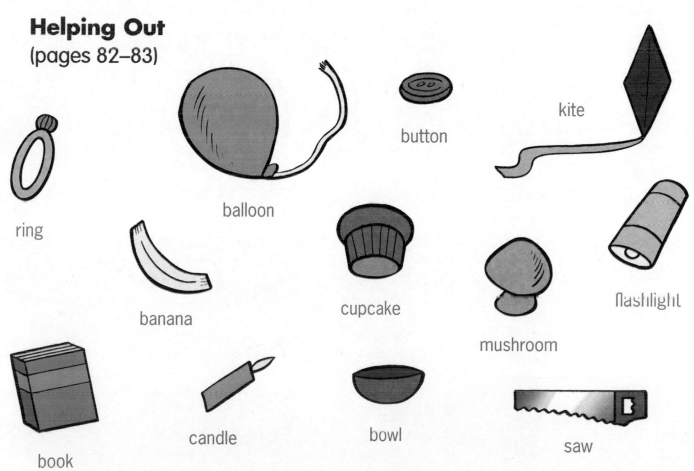

ring

balloon

button

kite

banana

cupcake

mushroom

flashlight

book

candle

bowl

saw

Highlights Highlights Highlights

Hidden Pictures Hidden Pictures Hidden Pi

Highlights Highlights Highli

Hidden Pictures Hidden Pictures Hidden P

Highlights Highlights Highli

Hidden Pictures Hidden Pictures Hidden Pi

Highlights Highlights Highlight

Hidden Pictures Hidden Pictures Hidden Pi

Highlights Highlights Highlig

Hidden Pictures Hidden Pictures Hidden Pi

Highlights Highlights Highli

Hidden Pictures Hidden Pictures Hidden Pi

ladder

button

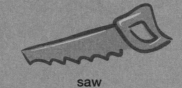
saw

banana

artist's brush

A Wheel Treat!

slice of pizza

football

cane

Illustrated by Dave Clegg

49

Illustrated by Ron Lieser

New Puppies

cookie

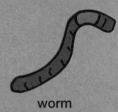
worm

drumstick

baseball bat

toothpaste

wristwatch

glove

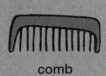
comb

54

ruler

carrot

spoon

crown

On Site

doughnut

pencil

magnet

spool of thread

Illustrated by David Coulson

A Perfect Pumpkin

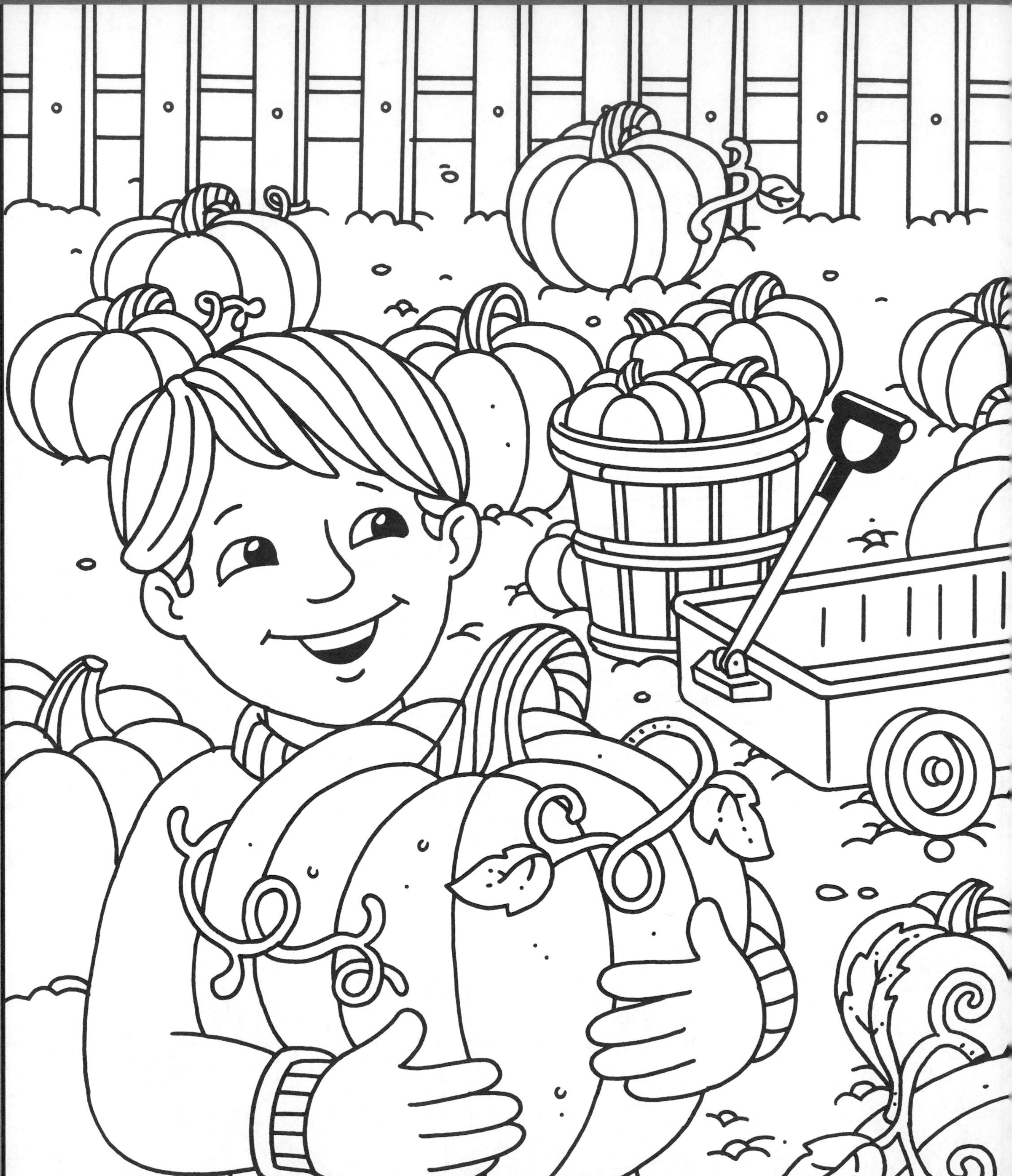

Illustrated by R. Michael Palan

Make-It Party

tomato

fried egg

envelope

slice of pizza

apple

comb

glove

crescent moon

60

hat

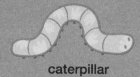
caterpillar

sock

slice of pizza

Up, Up, and Away

candy cane

basketball

stamp

horseshoe

Back and Forth

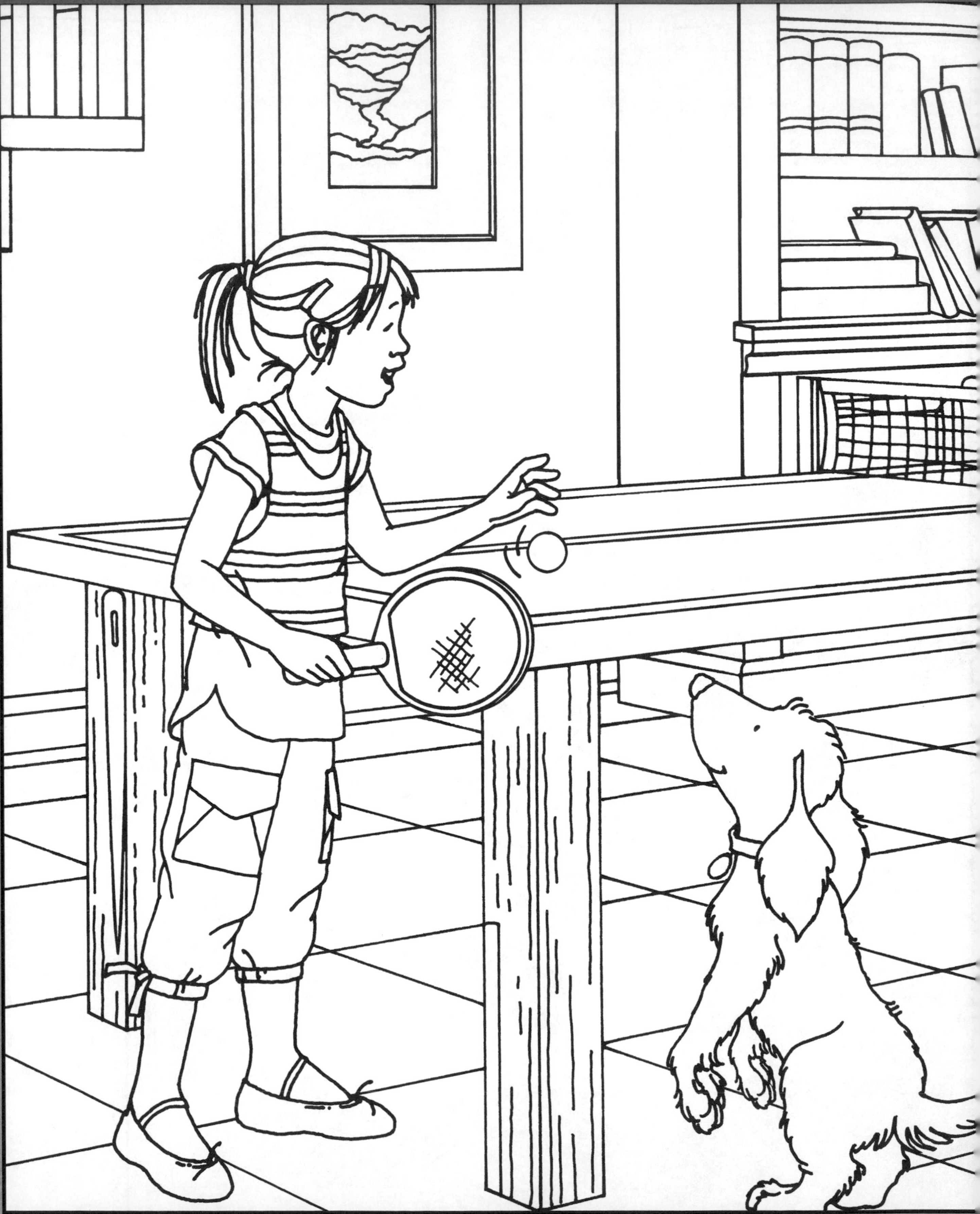

Frozen Fun

A Sky Surprise

drumstick

football

toothbrush

horseshoe

goldfish

notebook

meatball

pinwheel

lampshade

saltshaker

ladder

banana

glove

carrot

baseball bat

golf club

Tuning Up

Lots of Laces!

kite

slice of bread

fish

pencil

crown

seashell

scissors

book

Face Painting

slice of pizza

pear

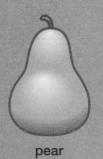

cupcake

Illustratec by Mark Collins

On the Farm

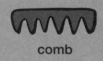

comb

sock

eyeglasses

cupcake

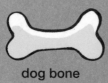

dog bone

apple

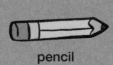

pencil

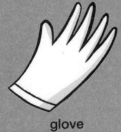

glove

72

canoe

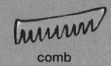
comb

carrot

caterpillar

Make a Wish!

crown

crayon

cane

cookie

Illustrated by Priscilla Burris

Camping Trip

crown

bell

pencil

crayon

sock

fish

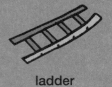
ladder

wishbone

78

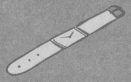

toothpaste

wristwatch

grapefruit

football

teacup

Batter Up!

cupcake

fishhook

pineapple

Just a Trim!

ice-cream bar

ladder

banana

cupcake

fish

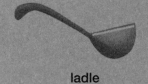
ladle

paper clip

leaf

mitten

flashlight

banana

drum

Dance Moves

kite

button

pencil

ball of yarn

Illustrated by Marilyn Janovitz

81

Illustrated by David Helton

Pass the Icing

mug

sailboat

crescent moon

pencil

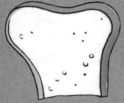
slice of bread

broccoli

football

turtle

84

lamp

sock

clock

butterfly

Duck Delivery

roll

stamp

slice of pie

bowl

Illustrated by Jamie Ho

85

Plane Ride

ladder

crescent moon

arrow

carrot

slice of pizza

fork

hammer

pencil

Answers

▼Pages 4–5

▼Page 6

▼Page 7

▼Pages 8–9

▼Pages 10–11

▼Page 12

Answers

▼Page 13

▼Page 14

▼Page 15

▼Pages 16–17

▼Page 18

▼Page 19

▼Pages 20–21

Answers

▼ Pages 22–23

▼ Page 24

▼ Page 25

▼ Pages 26–27

▼ Pages 28–29

▼ Page 30

Answers

▼ Page 31

▼ Pages 32–33

▼ Pages 34–35

▼ Page 36

▼ Page 37

▼ Pages 38–39

▼Pages 40–41

▼Page 42

▼Page 43

▼Pages 44–45

▼Pages 46–47

▼Page 48

Answers

▼ Page 49

▼ Pages 50–51

▼ Pages 52–53

▼ Page 54

▼ Page 55

▼ Pages 56–57

Answers

▼Pages 58–59

▼Page 60

▼Page 61

▼Pages 62–63

▼Pages 64–65

▼Page 66

Answers

▼ Page 67

▼ Pages 68–69

▼ Page 70

▼ Page 71

▼ Page 72

▼ Page 73

▼ Pages 74–75

Answers

▼ Pages 76–77

▼ Page 78

▼ Page 79

▼ Page 80

▼ Page 81

▼ Pages 82–83

▼ Page 84

Answers

▼ Page 85

▼ Page 86